EDWARD HOPPER

PAINTS HIS WORLD

For Jen—
You are the best!
—R. B.

Thanks to Dr. John Elefteriades,
who is a master of the art of cardiac medicine,
giving life and light to the human spirit
—W. M.

Henry Holt and Company, LLC, *Publishers since 1866*
175 Fifth Avenue, New York, New York 10010
mackids.com

Henry Holt® is a registered trademark of Henry Holt and Company, LLC.
Text copyright © 2014 by Robert Burleigh
Illustrations copyright © 2014 by Wendell Minor
All rights reserved.

Library of Congress Cataloging-in-Publication Data
Burleigh, Robert.
Edward Hopper paints his world / Robert Burleigh ; paintings by Wendell Minor.
pages   cm
ISBN 978-0-8050-8752-9 (hardback)
1. Hopper, Edward, 1882–1967–Juvenile literature. 2. Painters–United States–Biography–
Juvenile literature. I. Minor, Wendell, illustrator. II. Title.
ND237.H75B87 2014   759.13–dc23   [B]   2013037068

Henry Holt books may be purchased for business or promotional use. For information on
bulk purchases, please contact Macmillan Corporate and Premium Sales Department at
(800) 221-7945 x5442 or by e-mail at specialmarkets@macmillan.com.

First Edition—2014 / Designed by Wendell Minor and April Ward
The artist used gouache watercolor on Strathmore 500 Bristol
paper to create the illustrations for this book.

Printed in China by South China Printing Co. Ltd., Dongguan City, Guangdong Province

1 3 5 7 9 10 8 6 4 2

EDWARD HOPPER
PAINTS HIS WORLD

Robert Burleigh

Paintings by Wendell Minor

Christy Ottaviano Books

HENRY HOLT AND COMPANY • NEW YORK

Little Edward Hopper had many dreams. But one dream was biggest of all—he was going to be a painter when he grew up. On the cover of his pencil box, he printed these bold words: "WOULD BE ARTIST."

Edward drew and drew. He often gazed at the nearby Hudson River from his bedroom window, a drawing pad on his desk. Moving his pencil carefully, he would watch a sailboat, or a seagull, slowly emerge on the page. Magical! Sometimes he signed his youthful drawings like adult artists do—with his name in the lower corner: *Edward Hopper*

Tall and gangly, Edward grew quickly. His teasing
schoolmates called him "Grasshopper" because of his
long, thin legs.

While other boys played baseball or ran races,
Edward often walked to the riverbank to draw. The
sunlight on the water's rippling surface was so beautiful.
Still, to paint it exactly as it looked—that was hard.
Edward wondered: Will I ever be able to paint things
the way they appear to me?

After high school, Edward set off for New York City
to study illustration and painting. What an amazing time
it was: the beginning of the twentieth century. The great,
lively metropolis buzzed with excitement and possibilities.
Edward Hopper, filled with hope, felt he was becoming
a real artist at last. He took classes. He studied. He worked.

But to become the painter he wanted to be, Edward needed to learn even more. Paris called out to him. It was home to some of the world's most famous artists. Edward's trip to Paris opened a universe of new thoughts about painting. Always shy, he made few close friends on his travels. Yet he did make friends with many works of art, visiting museums and staring for hours at the pictures he found there.

He took time to paint outdoors, too. "The light and shadows of Paris," he wrote, "are different from anything I have ever known."

Brimming with ideas for pictures, Edward returned to
New York. He took a job illustrating for magazines, where
some of his illustrations won prizes. Even so, he wasn't happy
drawing pictures that others told him to draw. He wanted to
paint the subjects that moved him deeply. But how?

To save money, he rented an inexpensive apartment on
the top floor of an old building. His rooms were heated
only by a single stove, which he filled with coal he hauled
up each day from the basement. The bathroom wasn't even
in the apartment—it was down the hall. But who cared?
There was space for him to paint.

America was changing, and Edward
was eager to make art in a fresh, new
American way. There was one big problem:
No one wanted to buy his paintings.
Still, he didn't give up.

Because he was fascinated by the look and feel of old houses, Edward began to make paintings of them. Once he remarked: "All I want to do is paint sunlight on the side of a house."

But maybe Edward liked to paint houses for another reason. Many houses in his paintings seem moody, quiet, and alone. Were Edward's houses a bit like Edward himself?

When he was nearly forty-two years old, he married another artist. Her name was Jo Nivison. Years before, Edward and Jo had been fellow students in art school.

Jo gave Edward love, encouragement, and support.
She was the model for most of the women in his paintings.
She kept a careful diary, explaining how he created his
work. And along with Edward, she loved reading poetry,
going to plays, and watching movies.

They worked together, too. Sometimes they
drove into the country, where they painted in
the open air. If the weather was bad, they even
painted in the car.

At other times, they drove north along the Atlantic Coast, where Edward often painted the lighthouses they saw along the way. His lighthouse paintings are among his most beautiful works. The paint glows. The tall lighthouses rise up, gleaming in the sunlight, looming above land and sea.

Jo and Edward later built a small cottage by the bay on Cape Cod, Massachusetts, where they spent summers working and relaxing. Here, Edward painted many pictures of the sea.

As he drove through the nearby countryside, Edward stayed
on the lookout for scenes that moved him: not pretty gardens
and pleasant farms—but lonely roads, deserted buildings, or
dying businesses.

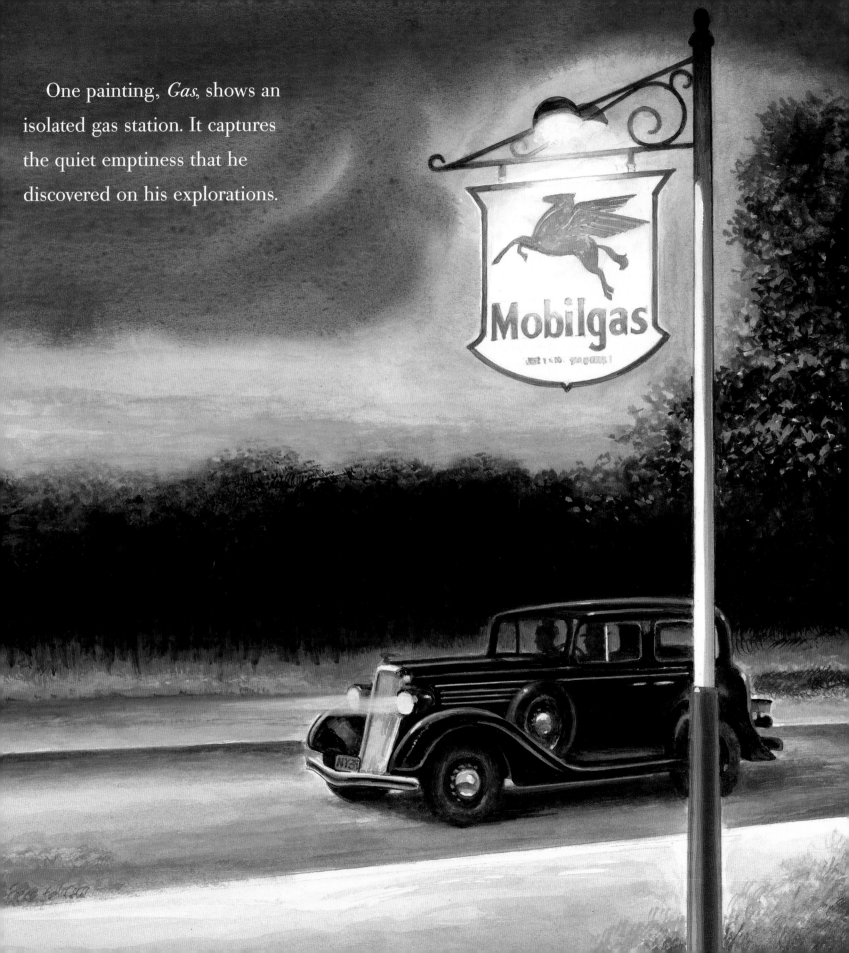

One painting, *Gas*, shows an isolated gas station. It captures the quiet emptiness that he discovered on his explorations.

Yet Edward Hopper still loved the city. He spent
many hours walking through New York streets. And
as always, he was searching.

He was looking for what other artists didn't paint.
He wanted to paint what others didn't see. Edward
wanted to paint what only *he* saw.

Wandering through the city, sketchbook in hand, he looked and looked. He saw faces staring out from upstairs windows. He saw a bored usher standing quietly in the lobby of a movie theater. He saw a weathered storefront in the stillness of an early Sunday morning.

He brought his sketches back to his studio, where he worked patiently. Sometimes he took weeks to complete a single painting.

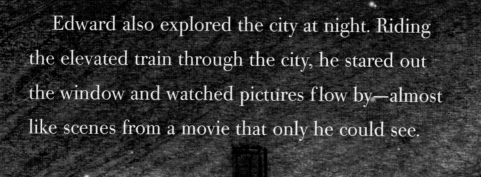

Edward also explored the city at night. Riding the elevated train through the city, he stared out the window and watched pictures flow by—almost like scenes from a movie that only he could see.

There, a couple reading in their living room. There, a man working late in a dim office. There, a lonely stroller on a dark street. Often, the people were serious. They seemed slightly sad. What had happened to them? What was about to happen? These small mysteries became the subjects for many of Edward Hopper's paintings.

But Edward didn't just copy what he saw. His paintings
often *combined* things he sketched on his travels: a café on
a deserted street corner, customers drinking coffee, lost in
thought—or dark shadows on an eerie green pavement.

Starting with scenes and details like these, Edward used
his imagination to create some of his best-known pictures.
One famous painting shows solitary people sitting at a counter
in an all-night diner. The painting is called *Nighthawks*.

"I was painting the loneliness of a large city," he later explained.

As the years passed, more people saw Edward's paintings.
Museums wanted to display his work. Critics began to see
something strange and wonderful in his pictures. But Edward
and Jo continued to live simply in their cottage on Cape Cod
or in their New York apartment. And Edward—as always—
continued to paint.

Once someone asked Edward why he painted. He paused
a moment. "Why do I paint? Well," he finally answered, "I'm
after ME." Yes, Edward wanted his paintings to show what he
saw, what he felt, and who he really was.

One of his last works is *Sun in an Empty Room.* We see a room with light pouring through a window. Nothing more. All is calm. All is still.

Was Edward satisfied at last? Whether it was lighthouses, people in lonely diners, or simply light on a wall, Edward Hopper had searched for, discovered—and painted—his special world.

AFTERWORD

EDWARD HOPPER: HERO, EXPLORER, AND ARTIST

Can an artist be a *hero*? We think of heroes as those who fight against great odds because they believe in a cause. If a hero is someone who holds true to his own vision despite many hardships, Edward Hopper was one. It takes courage to continue to work in difficult conditions without support or hope of recognition. Hopper's artistic path was long. Although he wanted to be an artist from childhood, he worked for many years before he found success. He continued making the paintings he believed in, living cheaply, getting little encouragement except from his wife, Jo. Even after finally receiving recognition from the art world, little changed for Edward Hopper. Quietly, patiently, he worked on.

Can an artist be an *explorer*? We think of explorers as those who break new ground and open up new territory. Hopper lived during a time of big changes in American and European art. Many artists were investigating new possibilities in art movements, like Cubism, Dadaism, and Surrealism. In addition, the rise of abstract art called into question the kind of painting that Hopper loved. But Hopper discovered and explored new art territory of his own, developing his unique vision in his portrayals of solitary people, the mysterious sea, shadowy rural landscapes, deserted city streets, empty houses, and lonely roads. When we look carefully, all these paintings say one thing: Edward Hopper—hero and explorer—was here.

HOPPER ON ART

Edward Hopper thought about art all his life. But he was a quiet man, and his comments on art were few. Jo Hopper once said, "Sometimes talking with Eddie is just like dropping a stone in a well, except that it doesn't thump when it hits bottom!"
  Here are a few things Edward said about art:

Great art is the outward expression of an inner life in the artist.
  He also said the same thing another way: "I'm after ME."
  He meant that a good artist is always trying to express in a picture what he or she believes is important in life.

If you could say it in words there would be no reason to paint.
  Edward is saying that painting is its own special way of telling the viewer something about life and beauty— painting is a language of its own.

In every artist's development, the germ of the later work is always found in the earlier.
  According to Edward Hopper, all artists use and build on the skills and thoughts that they had earlier, even as young artists. In the same way, an athlete becomes better by building on his or her special skills.

FOUR HOPPER PAINTINGS

EARLY SUNDAY MORNING

In this painting, Hopper depicts a deserted New York street. Only the squat hydrant and slightly tilted barber pole contrast with the many horizontal and vertical lines around which the picture is built. Where are the people? With no one in sight, the street seems to take on a quietness all its own.

[© Heirs of Josephine N. Hopper, licensed by the Whitney Museum of American Art]

LIGHTHOUSE HILL

A lighthouse, lit up by the sun, stands tall against a clear blue sky. Yet the house beside it is uninviting, and the shadows on the hillside are dark and forbidding. Is the lighthouse a kind of symbol of Hopper himself, who in 1927 when he painted this scene, was struggling to find his place in the art world? With its dramatic light and shadow, *Lighthouse Hill* remains a beautiful example of the artist's many coastal and rural paintings.

[Dallas Museum of Art]

GAS

It is late in the day, and the woods loom darkly over this lonely, brightly lit outpost at nature's edge. No cars approach. The gas station worker (dressed in business clothes) appears to be putting things away. The painting, called *Gas,* seems to be a simple scene of a gas station at twilight—but with Hopper, nothing is simple. What story does the painting tell?

[Mrs. Simon Guggenheim Fund/Museum of Modern Art]

NIGHTHAWKS

The most famous of Hopper's paintings, *Nighthawks* captures the feeling of a city late at night. Light streams through the glass windows of the diner onto the street outside, while three people sit at the counter, each lost in solitude. Who are they? Why are they there? Perhaps the painting is attempting to depict the loneliness of a large city.

[Friends of American Art Collection/The Art Institute of Chicago]

IMPORTANT DATES IN THE LIFE OF EDWARD HOPPER

EDWARD HOPPER was born on July 22, 1882, in Nyack, New York. In the early 1900s, Hopper studied art in New York and made several brief trips to Europe. In 1906, he began working in New York City as an illustrator while doing his own artwork on the side. In 1924, he married artist Jo Nivison, and the late 1920s, he quit commercial illustration and began to sell more of his work as his artistic reputation grew. Hopper painted many of his most famous paintings, including *Early Sunday Morning, Gas,* and *Nighthawks,* between 1930 and 1945. He received numerous prizes and awards for his art in the late 1940 and 1950s, including being elected to the American Academy of Arts and Letters in 1955. Edward Hopper died peacefully in his studio on May 15, 1967.

AUTHOR'S REFERENCES: HOPPER BIBLIOGRAPHY

There are many books dealing with the life and works of Edward Hopper. Here are just a few of them.

Berman, Avis. *Edward Hopper's New York* (Petaluma, CA: Pomegranate Press), 2005.

Levin, Gail. *Edward Hopper: An Intimate Biography* (Berkeley, CA: University of California Press), 1998.

Rubin, Susan Goldman. *Edward Hopper: Painter of Light and Shadow* (New York: Harry N. Abrams), 2007.

Spring, Justin. *The Essential Edward Hopper* (New York: Harry N. Abrams), 1998.

Troyen, Carol, et al. *Edward Hopper* (Boston, MA: Boston Museum of Fine Arts), 2007.

Wells, Walter. *Silent Theater: The Art of Edward Hopper* (London: Phaidon Press), 2007.

ARTIST'S REFERENCE SOURCES

Levin, Gail. *Edward Hopper: A Catalogue Raisonné,* volumes 1 through 3 (New York: W. W. Norton), 2003.

——. *Edward Hopper: An Intimate Biography* (Berkeley, CA: University of California Press), 1998.

——. *Edward Hopper as Illustrator* (New York: W. W. Norton), 1979.

——. *Hopper's Places* (Berkeley, CA: University of California Press), 1998.

Little, Carl. *Edward Hopper's New England* (Petaluma, CA: Pomegranate Press), 2011.

Mecklenburg, Virginia M. *Edward Hopper: The Watercolors* (New York: W. W. Norton), 1999.

Salatino, Kevin, et al. *Edward Hopper's Maine* (New York: Prestel Publishing), 2011.

WEBSITE SOURCES

The Whitney Museum: http://whitney.org

The Art Institute of Chicago: http://www.artic.edu/

The Museum of Modern Art: http://www.moma.org/explore/collection/

The Metropolitan Museum of Art: http://www.metmuseum.org/

Edward Hopper House Art Center: http://www.edwardhopperhouse.org/

ARTIST'S NOTE ON IMAGES IN THIS BOOK

Edward Hopper is one of the most important American artists of the twentieth century. Ever since I was a student, Edward Hopper has influenced my approach to the use of light, color, and composition. In this book, I tried to create the feeling of Hopper's art while maintaining my own style. Upon careful observation, the reader will notice many differences in my interpretations of four famous Hopper paintings in this book. My idea was to evoke the familiar through Hopper's point of view. You may often hear someone say of a particular scene, "That looks like a Hopper!"

In this book, Robert Burleigh and I have attempted to give the young reader an introduction to the artist's process of discovery. We see Hopper observing subjects, and we try to imagine what it might have been like to be there with him. Hopper sometimes sketched and painted his subjects on-site, but other times, he would return to his studio and sketch his observations from memory. His work is a combination of the real and the imagined. The best example of this is perhaps his most famous painting, *Nighthawks*. My research has shown that the all-night café in his painting never really existed. Hopper created this imaginary place from the many different scenes he encountered on his walks through New York City's streets—and he did it in such a way that the viewer is convinced they know this café to be real. Such is the power of creativity! Robert Burleigh and I hope that we will inspire young artists everywhere to observe and then create wonderful pictures of their world.

I would like to give special thanks to art historian and author Gail Levin
for taking such an interest in this book. Dr. Levin's expert guidance, along with
information provided in her book, *Edward Hopper: An Intimate Biography*,
gave me a sense of Hopper the artist that is truly unique.

—W. M.